Disposable Darlings

poems by Todd Cirillo

ROADSIDE PRESS

Cover Photograph: Carrie DeMay www.carriedemay.com
Cover Graphic Design: Julie Valin www.selftoshelfpublishing.com
To Linzi Garcia, Thank you.
Editor: Michele McDannold

Variations of many of these poems have previously appeared in: Black Shamrock, Hobo Camp Review, Heroin Love Songs, 48th Street Press, In Between Hangovers, Fearless, River Dog Zine #2, Elephant, The Daily Dope Fiend, Literary Corner New York Parrot, Rust Belt Review, Trampoline, Asylum Floor, Passion of Poetry, Rogue Wolf Press, Scattergun Poetry Journal, The Rye Whiskey Review and Horror, Sleaze, Trash

Roadside Press
Meredosia, Illinois

Table of Contents

To Carey Floyd

who will always be welcome at my door.

"There he goes. One of God's own prototypes. A high-powered mutant of some kind never even considered for mass production. Too weird to live, and too rare to die."—Dr. Hunter S. Thompson

Magnolias

On top of him
he focuses on her quick breaths,
the rhythm of her body
her hands tightening,
the side-to-side of her hip bones,
hair falling off the shoulders,
the curve of the ribs
holding her enthusiastic heart,
eyes lowered
to his.

It is spring,
the jasmine are in bloom outside
along with the magnolias she loves so.
With a hushed voice
she tells him,
I like that.

He kisses the inside
of her left wrist
knowing every spring
he has now
will feel like
her.

Poetry Suckers

I am proofreading
her book of poems
which will be published
this year
and smiling at all the idiot men
who will read it
while seriously believing
that the poems
in the book
are all about them.

But I know
who they are really about—
at least that's what
I tell myself.

True Love

Eventually,
I missed
even
the lies
she told
me.

Do You Know That Feeling?

Do you know that feeling
when a relationship
reaches a point
where you just smile
at the ease and comfort of it all?

When conversations come easily
and you talk all the time
about the weather,
the news of the day,
the state of the country,
places to go and see,
what to add to grocery lists,
books you are reading
or dumb jokes you tell each other
that aren't necessarily funny
but you laugh anyway
because you just appreciate the effort.

You find the ways
in which you complement one another,
like one is better at math or spelling
or the other plays the perfect music
while cooking.

That is not to say,
there are no challenging times
or breakdowns in communication
where you can go a day or two
without being able to speak
to each other.

I've heard that in every relationship
there are times when you
have to simply take a break
and recharge.

But that is where the reliability
and comfort comes in.
They say it takes time to get to that point.
However, they also say,
at other times
it just happens instantly.

And this is how my
latest relationship began.

I met her online,
it seems to be the only option these days,
I haven't introduced her
to many of my close friends yet,
a few have met her,
but we are still figuring one another out,
how to respond to one another,
how to make this work,
though I am optimistic
and it already feels comfortable.

My favorite part though,
are those slow-moving mornings,
when my arm rests
under the cool side of the pillow,
birds make bird sounds in the courtyard
just beyond the windows
and she greets me with,
Good morning, Todd,
and I like how she annunciates my name,
and that she is there,
so I turn in the bed
to greet her as well,
Good morning, Alexa,
what is the weather today?

Slut Shaming

It was a wild one.
That much I know.
Now, first light of morning,
unclear how we arrived
in these unfamiliar surroundings,
clear on what happened though,
clearer still on the consequences
that await,
trying to be quiet,
I say out loud,
"You fucking slut,"
as I wash my face,
avoiding the mirror.

A Romantic Gesture

I came across your name
written in cement—
a romantic gesture
of long ago.
A faded time
when hope appeared
as a possibility.

Your name
has been
stepped on,
driven over,
puked and pissed on,
until the "e" at the end
is now barely recognizable.

Standing over it
seeing you slowly disappearing
piece by piece,
letter by letter,
it is another crack in the sidewalk
for me
to step over.

True Legend
—*for Carey Floyd*

He is up in Alaska cooking
on a fishing boat
that never leaves the dock.
It is his ten thousandth
short-term job
in a decade stacked up
with short-term jobs.
They get fewer and far between
as his smoking, drinking and isolation
grows deeper.
We always text back and forth
yet, I always worry about him.
He spends most days alone,
though he has survived
more than most could ever imagine.
Always broke
but never broke down.
Those who know him
tell stories at parties and pool tables,
the time he drank seven hand grenades
from Bourbon Street,
or when he left a party at eleven
and came back at four in the morning
with someone else's clothes on,
his word-for-word knowledge of biblical verse,
or the moment he announced,
at the stuffy Uptown garden party:
"If I knew it was this type of party,
I'd have stuck my dick in the mashed potatoes."
I miss him and wonder if he ever feels disheartened.
I ask,
"How's it goin' up there?"
He responds,
"Pretty good,

kind of sad,
the old Captain's wife passed away,
salmon are all dead this year,
lots of sitting around
making sure no one steals my stuff...
But, I learned how to make homemade lox today!"

Some legends
are just not that well known.

Saints of the Neons

It matters not
what bar, any bar,
any town, anywhere.
It is where us serious drinkers
talk shit
and gossip,
backslap
and bullshit
yet
hold one another tight
when it's necessary.
And if two weekends pass
we wonder
where you've been.
We've broken up
in front of the beer taps
and busted our faces
at happy hour
defending someone's honor.
We have seen kids
grow up
and marriages
grow old,
lives born
and lights
go out.

We've heard every jukebox tune
a thousand times,
sometimes in one sitting.
We have over-tipped
to be over-served.
Have woken up
with the hair of the dog
and passed out

when the sun
shows its face.
We have done shots
and been shot down.
Downed pints
and puked
in the garbage cans.

Embarrassed
and absolved ourselves
over Jaeger bombs
and Bloody Marys.

Here, we are equal—
equally lost
equally broke
equally off
and we look almost innocent
under the neons.

We spend hungover holidays
on barstool thrones,
where liquor bottles
stand like gods
under Christmas lights
providing us gifts
we didn't know
we needed.

Even though Sunday mornings
can be brutal
without a hint
of redemption,
we crawl back
to the neons
full of confessions and contrition,
where we never have to order,

the bartender simply has it waiting
with a beerback of forgiveness
and that feels
better than church
to saints like us.

Making It Right

In the morning
just as the first peek of sun
squeezes through the blinds
you are still here
a little spoon
curled into me
smiling
making the world
right enough
to forget
such a thing as
goodbye
ever existed.

Natural Disaster

Black Rebel Motorcycle Club
appeared on my Spotify shuffle today.
The record that came out
when we were orbiting
each other.
In between those times
and today,
there have been hurricanes,
earthquakes, floods,
fires, tsunamis,
volcanic eruptions,
epidemics and outbreaks.
Natural disasters
of every style and magnitude.
The music causes ripples and waves
of us then and the us now.
How we will never speak again
is another natural disaster
in the history of this world.

Luckenbach, Texas

I have reached the point
of becoming
a goddamn country music cliché.
I sit alone
in a dirty bar
in ripped jeans, trucker hat,
light wallet
surrounded by
old, torn posters,
faded chalk board,
blinking half-neons,
a dusty bottle of root beer Schnapps
not touched since '78
and busted dreams
drinking cheap beer and strong shots
listening to
Waylon Jennings
sing about
Willie and the boys
and
I know
all the
words.

These kinds of situations
make a person reflective.
I realize my life contains
most of the classic elements,
wrecked trucks by loves
long lost,
stranded in the rain
without bus fare
and no way home,
thrown in jail three times
for things I was completely

guilty of,
been cheated out of my money
and my heart,
left for other men,
and, if I'm being honest,
the occasional woman too,
had all the light bulbs in my house
methodically busted out
one by one,

had a shotgun pointed
in my face
and when she said it was loaded,
I took her word for it.
But I don't ride horses,
wear a giant bucking bronco belt buckle
or even own a dog.

Yet, here I sit
at the far end
of the bar
with an open tab,
living it up
writing the next chorus.
Just me,
Waylon,
Willie
and the
boys.

Kick Out the Jams Motherfucker

—for Julie Valin

She keeps going back
to the blues.
When I want her
to be Rock N Roll,
Punk's early days,
Grunge
and Heavy Metal thunder.
I simply want her
to quit fucking around,
kick out the jams
and put her stories down
onto the page.
To get those words
out to the masses.
But she doesn't want to be a frontwoman
swinging the microphone centerstage,
frontpage of all the magazines,
busting heads,
hearts and guitar strings.
She simply wants to hold onto
the slow rhythm
of back porch blues
with a melody
that doesn't burn out
or fade away
but drifts across the years
until eventually everyone hears it
and realizes
this is where it all began.

Center of the Universe

—the secret life of poets

Sometimes,
I can't even
read my own poetry....

sometimes.

The Cosmic Jukebox

I am done
believing in signs.
Those moments we think
bring us together.

All the hope we place
upon this sign or that one;
you both wanted the same wedding song,
scars on the left knee,
a love of baseball,
the way you both stare
so fucking deeply into one another,
never breaking that sight line
because it is meant to be.

However,
my experience has been
that the chaotic fuckedupness
of the universe
has paid out
more times than signs
ever have.

Although...
there is one sign,
the *only* sign
that seems to appear,
without fail,
at the exact moment of meaning.
It is the string of
sad, lonely songs
that will randomly play
anywhere and everywhere
and ALWAYS
after a breakup.
That is a sure thing.

It is the songs that stay with us,
follow us, tease and torture us.
And always when we finally
get that person
out of our waking thoughts
and we feel confident enough
to start again,
looking for signs
and sure things.

I'll stick with the random fuckedupness
and take what presents itself:
the good
the smiles
the touch
the illusion
and the twisted
cosmic jukebox
that plays and plays—
no dollars
required.

Worth the Wait

Waiting for you
to board a plane,
find your seat,
buckle in
and head
into the sky
land in Houston
wait out
a 2 ½ hour layover
board another plane,
find another seat
and arrive back home—
here in New Orleans
where even at 1:24 a.m.
you will find
live music, open bars,
laughter,
a river rolling
and a heart
that has been waiting
to say
welcome home.

Useful Poetry

I read the poet's new book
and saw this line,
Waiting for something
Hoping for anything.
It is the type of brilliant phrase
that will stick with people
when they read it
on buses and trains,
if people still used
buses and trains.
But I am confident
that this book
will be read in airports
by people going to see other people
or those who are getting away
from everyone.
It will have significance
during break-ups
and given as gifts
to impress.
It will be quoted at weddings
and funerals,
lines will be stolen
by those who call themselves poets.
It will be opened over and over
again and again
and it will be opened only once
and placed on a shelf with other books
with crisp spines and unstained pages.
Don't take it personally—
pages will also get covered in
gin and tonics, baby food,
spaghetti sauce, birthday cake,
dark chocolate, red wine,
and white russians.

Other times,
this book will solve problems—
an unbalanced pool table,
or crooked washing machine.
Don't take that part personally either,
it may not be what you hoped for,
but just remember, poetry is supposed
to be useful.

Down on the Corner

I watch the couple
standing on the corner.
She leans deep into him,
as if sculpted there
by their own dreams
and hopes.
The sky pure blue,
the sun burning heavily overhead.
There is no crying today,
not a hint of winter on its way.
Only the sun, sky
and a girl
leaning against a boy
as I drive past.

Wishful Thinking

We kissed once.
It was on the corner
of Rampart Street and St. Peter
in New Orleans.
I wish I could say
it was that magic
movie moment,
with the perfect song,
perfect set up,
lighting just right,
bright orange moon overhead,
anticipation giving way
to action,
like the final scene
in Sixteen Candles,
with the two main characters
kissing on a table,
birthday cake shining
with lit candles in between
with nothing left to wish for.
And when the credits rolled
everyone was already halfway home,
satisfied and happy
with what the stars
brought to them.

But our kiss wasn't like that.
It was sloppy,
we were drunk,
the music sucked,
there was spilled beer
and strangers crowding our space.
We could not really call it
romantic.
We could only admit

it happened
once.
There have been no second chances.

I have had
a thousand more moments
between that kiss and today,
some amazing,
others incredible,
fulfilling and fun—
but all have put me
back here,
alone,
staring at the stars,
with just one wish left.

Past Life of a Pirate

Sitting on a deck
having lunch,
reading poems.
I hear parrots
somewhere above me.
I look up,
then around,
this way and back
unable to spot them
but they call out.
It must be the pirate part
of my personality
that attracts them.
Teasing me with reminders
of what I could have gotten away with.
Their songs and squawks
cause me to drift and float away
to ports of palm trees and sea breezes,
hidden treasures,
a map full of x's
that I've never found
but feel like
home.

Edges

In bed
there are no barriers
only flesh.
I press my face
in between
the blades of your shoulders
and the points
of your edged hip bones.

I've never been afraid
of sharp things.

Lawrence Ferlinghetti Is Smiling

The poet and publisher,
Lawrence Ferlinghetti,
has died.
One hundred and one years
of stories, one in a million
moments and memories
stored in his
Coney Island mind,
gone with him.
Forever lost.
A chapter has ended.
For the literary world
it is sadness.

But, I bet he's smiling
considering it a respite
from sixty-eight long years
of opening the daily mail
to terrible poets
sending their best bad poetry
with hand written notes
howling to him
about how they
are the next big thing.

Feeling Good Enough

It is mid-day
and I am leaving
my house
for the first time today.
I have worked on old poems,
cleaned out ashtrays,
crushed the beer cans,
swept the broken bottles,
tucked away
cocktail napkin phone numbers
of last night's adventures
and am headed to lunch
to work on new poems.

I cross Coliseum Square Park
where gangs of old ladies
in clean white dresses
step in and out of mansions
professionally decorated for the holidays.
They have each paid $50
for the Lower Garden District
Holiday Home Tour.
I watch as they carefully
step around the bums
in dirty brown blankets
surrounded by dirty brown bags,
no shoes on,
asleep in the grass
on broken cardboard beds.

There is a fountain,
and 300-year-old Live Oaks
covered in Spanish Moss
with squirrels and dogs
racing around.

I say hello
to a beautiful woman
staring at her phone
with a *High Voltage* AC/DC shirt on.
I catch her off guard,
by the time she responds
I am down the road.

Despite being this close
to Christmas,
it is t-shirt weather
and the sun greets us
like something precious,
as when someone gives you
the last beer in the cooler.

I find a place to sit outside and eat.
I watch the people
on Magazine Street
shopping, drinking,
taking selfies and holding hands
and feel good enough
to order a drink myself—
and another and another.

In fact,
I feel like the poet,
William Taylor Jr.
happy with everything
and anything
this day
has to offer.

I Should Have Just Gotten You a Card

In the weeks
leading up to her birthday
I paid close attention,
stealthily inquired,
wrote down ideas
of what she may want.
Eventually, I made surprise plans,
fun Amazon orders
and set up a big, bright bouquet
to be delivered the day of.
The night before
her birthday
she called
told me
she found someone new
and that is what she wanted.

The one thing
I hadn't thought of.

Dilemma

The danger
in asking
a bartender out
is the difference
between
free and full price.

The Poet vs. The Artists

Here I am,
sitting in a mansion
surrounded by true artists.
Well known musicians,
actors, geniuses,
even a world-renowned doctor!
They are collaborating, creating,
working off one another.
They sing, play guitar, improvise stories,
offer suggestions and critiques.
I watch their fingers move
with such grace and natural ability
up and down the neck of the guitar
like tiny waves
or snapping in perfect time
to the beat,
holding a pen just right,
so the words fill this entire room.
They are the smooth hands
of the artist.

I listen and stare,
nodding my head
each time someone looks my way
feigning understanding of their magic
running my fingers over the cuts
on my busted knuckles
and scarred left hand
wondering
how it comes so easily to them?
and is the beer free?

There's been people sitting
in this room for over 150 years
trying to get something out of these moments.

Could be love, could be laughter,
affection or affirmation
from an audience or a stranger,
a quick glance
we will remember for a lifetime,
to hum the tune we heard,
or laugh at the story we listened to
or get a number from someone
way out of our league...
or perhaps, even just something
to write about.

A good song
can be created spontaneously
by musicians
but a good poem
can never be constructed on the spot.
The poet can only get inspired
with maybe a decent line or two
but then must crawl off
like a dying animal
to craft the poem
alone.
That is why in poetry
there are no Lennon and McCartneys,
Page and Plant,
or Jagger/Richards.

Creating a good poem
is like magic,
the secret is in tricking people
into wondering how you did it.

So, I will just sit back,
finish this beer,
order another
to see if I get a bill

and think of a famous song
sung by famous artists
that said,
all you need is love
and if that's all I get out of this
that's good enough for me,
maybe even good enough
to head home,
alone,
and get a poem
out of it.

The Buddha of Last Call

At the end of the evening
I take two or three Ibuprofens
to clear my mind
of what could have been
or what never was
and all that I was holding on to.

The Golden Boy of the Midwest

While some patrons sat
at the bar
there he was
up onstage
reading his poems
about death, decay
the depression
of being raised by
a daddy
who didn't love him
enough.
Most of the audience up front
were shouting and yelling
in support,
crying and throwing their hands in the air
wanting more death,
begging for more decay,
popping their own antidepressants
and gathering material
for their new poems
about a daddy
who didn't love them
enough.

The rest of us
ordered another round
and hoped for death too—
but not
for the same reasons.

Relapse

A good friend
wrote a great poem
about the best girlfriend
I've had.
He sent me his new book
today,
and there it is,
her name right there
in fine black ink
like a bookmark,
page 87.

He thought she would appreciate
an autographed and inscribed copy—
and she will—
but he also thought I wouldn't mind
sending it along to her
across our worlds of separateness.

Ever the gentleman,
I now must contact her
and find the most delicate
way to get this book
into her hands.

I dial her number
and just like that,
three solid years of recovery
lost
at the sound
of her hello.

Parking Lot Love

After weeks
of flirtation,
brushing one another
on the pass-by,
engineering the seating arrangements
and moving closer
and closer,
we finally went for it
on the first night
that felt like true winter.
No sounds,
only stars
and the rings
on our fingers tapping
as we touched
then moved
into the kiss—
and then,
the loud screeching voice
of her downstairs neighbor
arriving in her
hunk of shit car
to match her character,
angry that I had parked
my new truck
in her old spot.
The moment broke,
leaving us apart
under the cold moon
saying goodbye
with a hug
and a hope
of another evening
when we can finish
what we started

because for now
passion is put on hold
in favor of parking regulations.

Making a Difference

I saw a poster
advertising
100,000 poets for change
was happening tonight.

I found a seat
near the stage,
and they began
to read their poems
in a lifeless way that did not
help their cause.
Most were about
homelessness,
mental illness
and economic down times.
I am not sure
what their poems
were trying to change
but they definitely needed help.
I reached deep
into my jean pockets—
threw everything I had at them
and walked out,

hoping to have made a difference.

Good Strategy

—for Wolfgang Carstens

There is a man
way up north,
beyond borders, plains,
and mountain ranges.
Without his beard he looks respectable
even—
harmless.
He has a wife,
mortgage, a snow blower,
more kids, bills, and responsibilities
than I will ever know.
I imagine him
at a mild-mannered job
maybe wearing a uniform,
stocking shelves.
A man working
peacefully within the system.
Volunteers for the graveyard shift
allowing the darker words
to form under the florescent glow
of aisle 9,
but at home
when the seal is broken,
the fridge is stocked,
and he is firing on all cylinders,
he is a motherfucking Mack truck
of a man
barreling through every barricade—
poetic and otherwise,
smoking, drinking,
making videos
of himself reading
tough and unforgiving
poems he has written.

Until it is time to punch in once again.

I can only sit back
in awe and admiration
at his brutal strategy
of total retaliation
against
ALL of it.

Concerned Citizen

Talking loudly,
she said into her phone,
"I don't want you
to think I'm stalking you
or anything,
but I was wondering
where you were."

I could not hear
his response
as she continued;
"I mean,
you haven't been
at your house
or answered any of my calls,
emails, Facebook messages
texts or tweets.
Don't you see...
I HAD to keep calling,
in case you were hurt."

After hanging up,
she exclaimed,
"oh shit"
and proceeded to
dial him back.
"I'm at the Three-Legged Dog
on Burgundy and Conti",
she told him,
since he obviously
forgot to ask.

The Deal

It used to be
that we had sympathy
for the devil—
a man of wealth and taste,
style, strength and substance,
something of notice.
When the devil wrote a song
or poem,
it stood out, way out
on the edge
like a dirt road
or dark alley.
It wore a black leather jacket
and ripped jeans,
smoked nonfiltered cigarettes
with a shot and a beer chaser,
eight-ball in the corner pocket,
carried that
someone's getting lucky tonight
swagger.
The words written
with diamond precision
and total indifference
of whether people took notice
or not,
but everyone always did.

The words were that good.

And when the devil
made an offer
you took it as a serious compliment.

Now, there is
sympathy for mediocrity.

The whole scene
gone viral,
blogs created,
words written casually
from safe spaces
with soft landings
but yelled
with suffering intent.

Everyone insisting
they have something important
to offer,
some secret knowledge:
how to live,
how to eat,
how to say hello,
how not to offend,
how to be cleaner,
how to write poetry,
how to be meaningful
or most righteous.

Whiny vanilla angels
offering weekly threats
of exiting social media
or life,
only to repost again
within minutes.
Putting out
new "art"
by the hour.
Naming themselves prolific
without care for
content or quality,
counting likes as Pulitzer Prizes,
Pushcart nominations as victories,
producing work that truly equals

all the other nominees
that bravely hit "post"
with their brand new,
unedited, first draft masterpieces.

I prefer to reserve my sympathy
for the devil
because the devil
maintains standards,
and never deals in mediocrity.
The devil remains
one of the rare ones
who, no matter the consequence,
always deals
in style, substance
and taste.

Dear Sweetheart

take comfort
in your absolute
poetic aloneness
while the right words
move inside you
to the beat
of your perfect song
at your perfect moment
and have the sense
to fall in love
again and again
with that moment
clear and clean
feeling absolutely alive
and necessary
limitless
and pure
as the blue sky
in front of you
which is more comfort
than I can ever give.

Skeletons

All my skeletons have names.
They do not live in closets but in places.

Most cities and towns in California,
Waikiki, New Orleans, Bend, Boulder,
Kansas City, Detroit, Cleveland,
Brooklyn, Morgan City, Tucson,
the bottom of the Grand Canyon,
the middle of Sequoia National Park,
some small side of the road town
I can't remember,
standing by a late-night jukebox in Seattle,
hot springs in the Bitterroot mountains,
a bike rental shop in Key West,
in front of lockers in high school hallways,
a week in the Rocky Mountains,
the Double Shot bar in New York City,
a campground in Moab,
stretch of highway between Lawrence and Kansas City,
a cold cabin by a lake in Ludington,
St. Charles Avenue during Mardi Gras
full of glitter and glass beads.

My skeletons do not wait
until Halloween to appear,
they are with me always.
They do not rattle their bones,
they shout with voices.
Each one demanding
my attention
with questions of,
Why? How could you?
What happened?
Didn't you want it to be better?

Since living in a graveyard
I've become comfortable
speaking with the skeletons
and
sometimes,
when I've heard enough
I even try
to give them answers.

What Little Remains

Another bar
where no one knows
my name,
yet the bartenders recognize me
from previous nights
I've dipped in.
It is the dead of winter—
a good time
of year
to go unnoticed.
Everyone facing
the night's chill
in their own way,
retreating
to their own warm corners,
a time for keeping
only the bare essentials
hidden under all the layers.
I clutch my glass
and hold tight
to what little remains.

Red Light

I am mesmerized
by the
red-headed girl
wearing a summer dress
of flowers
in springtime
crossing the avenue
at a red light.

I watch her
all the way across—
she may have winked
at me
or gave a slight wave.

All the way
I watch her
and forget the honking.
She is far on the other side
when I realize
I have missed
another
green light.

Intuition
—for Brenton Booth

After finishing his book
I wrote to him
to compliment a poem
that describes his time
with a certain prostitute.
He wrote back,
"thanks about the poem,
prostitutes can be nuts,
as you clearly know."

He and I have yet to meet.

Bent Corners

Everything we have
ever written
or read
to one another
is now marked
by bent corners
of a book
that has been shelved
and will rarely
be taken down.

But when it is,

we will read
those pages
with bent corners
reminding us
of all our best
parts.

My First Time

It is my first time
back in a bar
since the world shut down.
Over 394 days,
I haven't missed this many
happy hours and last calls
since I was 15.
I jump at the first opportunity
to pay someone else
top dollar
to make me a well drink
while I look around
hoping for those old inspirations...
lipstick, a flash of smile,
a moment of eye contact,
summer dress walking to or away,
brushing hair back behind the right ear,
slow moving finger
over the top of a glass,
swaying hips at the jukebox.

A bartender
sits at a table,
six feet away,
smoking,
taking a break from trying,
trying to make back
all she lost
over the last year,
hoping people will be generous enough
to cover the months of back rent,
credit card debt
and overdue bills.

I stare at the smoke
of her cigarette
slowly rising up
from the cracked, black ashtray
towards the fat, white clouds above
leaving behind a signal
I can no longer read,
so I don't even notice
her
walking away—

christ,
it's been
a long year.

Al Green

Sitting together
in that uncomfortable space
between one more shot
and the last straw,
Al Green sings
Let's stay together
in the background.

There's a million lines
I could give voice to,
yet, I think,
if Al Green's
true soul voice
can't convince her—
then there's nothing
I'll ever be able to say.

So for once
I keep my mouth
shut.

The Side Hustle

The homeless man
a half block off Bourbon Street
rocks forward and back
in his wheelchair
begging passerbyes
on the street
for money.
The wheelchair
is an old rusted
and broken-spoked
deal, human powered.
He is similar,
filthy, ragged clothes,
a torn bandana around his neck
dirty hands and long fingernails
his right shoe
has no laces.
He mumbles to people
about how he served the country
and now the country
should serve him.
Most walk on by
but others reach in their pockets
to pull some coins
or a crisp buck
and place it into
the broken styrofoam cup
his shaking hands hold.
When the crowd
becomes few and far between
he calls it a night.
Takes the money out of the cup,
puts it into his pocket
gets up and walks away
into the night
all the richer.

The Luckiest Man Alive

Everyone says,
"Oh how lucky you are
to be on your own,
you can do whatever you want."

As I sit here,
alone,
typing
alone,
soon to sleep
alone,
soon to wake up
alone.

With all the luck in the world.

Passing the Time

Sitting with the old timers again—
mid-afternoon—
one of the last legitimate bars
left in town.
We stare at the games
on the TV,
gaze out the dirty windows,
play the occasional
classic rock song
on the jukebox
that reminds them all
of when they drove
tougher cars
and had hotter women.
Now they talk
about their women
and how they just don't compare
to that one chick they met
at the Grand Funk Railroad show
in 1976.
Some men don't talk about their women
at all, just Grand Funk Railroad.
They all flirt
with the afternoon shift bartender,
tell her she's still got it,
say that the evening bartender
with big tits, whose shift begins at 6 p.m.
is a bitch and can't pour a proper drink for shit.
They order their drinks
and nod to the music of long ago
and slowly fade away,
far away—
from inspiration,
from love,
from bills,

children
and eventually themselves,
and the sun begins to go down
on all of us
as the big-titted bartender's shift
crawls closer
and we all begin to sip our drinks a little slower,
saving our money for another round
after six.

What The Hell Am I Doin' Here?

Standing alone
jamming brand new dollar bills
into this broke down old jukebox.
Playing songs for you;
some Tom Waits, Otis Redding
hoping you'll hear them
even though
you're not around.

Every night I go to sleep
to dream you up.
Each morning
I wake up
and must have
just missed you.

> *I don't belong here,*
> *I wish I was special.*

I like to get dressed up
in my best shorts, bucket hat,
a semi-clean and clever t-shirt,
take my beach bum vibe and head out
looking for the heart of Saturday night,
even on a Wednesday.

Sometimes I wake up
before the sun comes up,
check my pockets
for numbers and possibilities.
Usually I find,
a pocketful of lonesome
and half-written love poems.

> *I wish those were special*
> *So very special.*

Mostly, I just wander alone
walking these busted streets
searching for pretty things to say,
listening to songs for ghosts,
wishing on stars,
trying to hold on to that memory of her.

But, I've decided to stop wishing
on stars,
it is too sad
to watch them go out
slowly one by one by one.
I've tried rainbows
but they are so hard to catch.

> *I just wish I was special.*
> *So very special.*

I am not saying everything
turned out wrong
but it most definitely
is not right.
It is like repeatedly
going on first dates
that no one shows up to.
Maybe someone will notice,
I want you to notice.

> *That would make me special*
> *So very, very special.*
> *So fucking special.*

Together

They take pictures
in the exact spot
they did five years ago.
So much has changed.
Their smiles
remain.

Saturday Night Sounds

The well-dressed
gang of girls
sit at the outside table
smoking cigarettes slowly
in their high boots,
tight skirts,
taking bored selfies
and watching the streetcars
pass down St. Charles Avenue.

Occasionally, one of them
looks up at the stars,
which are covered
by the grey sky,
but she continues
to stare
as if willing the clouds
away.

A saxophone begins to blow
a half block down the street,
the rest of the group
doesn't even look
towards the beauty
of Saturday sound,
and the star watcher
continues to gaze upwards.
The sax man walks our way
playing his heart out loudly.
He passes the outside tables
and drowns out
the Kanye West
coming from the inside jukebox.

When he passes
and his Saturday sounds
begin to blend
with the noises of evening,
the stargazer looks
from sky to saxophone,
appears to sway
in her seat,
slaps her hands on the table
and announces to her friends,

"Let's get fucked up!"

and who can argue
with that?

Of the Moment

The kids
scream and yell
on the playground.
I yell with them,
just not as loud.
They are wild
under a sky of fat clouds.
I am wild
just not as wild anymore.

The swings creak and squeak
sounding the same on any playground
anywhere.
The kids run up slides,
dodge a ball,
run from a tag,
hide from a seek.
The winners stand, arms raised up
smiling as kings of the playground,
champions of the moment.

I watch all of this
and when the kids are gone
I run up the slide
and stand atop, arms raised
like a champion—
still king
of the moment.

Your First

That first drink
of the evening
still reminds me
of the original one.
Fourteen years old.
The warmth from the throat
to the chest
deep with mystery
and mischief
from a time
when you could indulge
in mischief and get away
with it.
Back when you never truly
enjoyed the sip
but loved what comes after.
I still smile
holding the glass
and moving it in slow circles,
the ice cubes knocking
against the side
like a secret song,
or watching the bartender
tip the bottle
completely vertical
putting distance between it
and the glass—
all that mystery
of what's to come
served with a tiny straw.

I've since done things
that no one has noticed—
guess I am
still getting away with it.

Moving In

There are
four chambers
to the human heart.
You have
moved into
each one
of mine.

I hope you relax,
stay awhile,
get comfortable,
feel free to leave a toothbrush,
some clothes,
your favorite books
anything you like.
No need to clear anything out,
there is plenty of space.

The place hasn't
been lived in
for years.

Souvenirs

Nowadays,
all those loves,
those real attempts
sit like souvenirs
on a high shelf
with memories and moments
piled up around them,
taking up space.

I take them down
and dust them off
every once in awhile
and hold them tightly
letting the big feelings
wash over me
like a rainstorm,
trying to get back to those places.

But souvenirs are just things
we hold on to
from places and people
that fade away in time.
And besides,
who wants to be surrounded
by reminders
of all the pretty places
we will never return to
again?

Stacking the Deck

I notice that,
at the end of our conversations
he always says,
Love ya.
This is a fairly recent addition
to our talks.
He is much older than I am
and we have known one another
for over twenty years now.
I am a writer
and he is a writer.
It is the way it sounds
that catches me off guard,
even now.
He proclaims it
with honesty, conviction and clarity.
No jokes,
no curse words
hiding it,
no hesitation,
no bullshit—
just like him.

It feels like
something he wants to just
slip into the conversation,
no need to make a big deal
of it.

Truth be told,
the phrase makes me feel good
and I hope it makes him
feel even better.
So, I roll with it
and always reply,

Love ya too.
It is an all too rare moment
between men with the type of scars
he and I have.
A connection.

However, each time
he says it,
I can't help but wonder how or why
he added this endearment
and affection.
What prompted this?
Why is he saying it NOW?
Perhaps it is his age.
I have noticed
the cracks in his voice of late,
the slowing down he speaks about.
He even wrote an entire book
about getting old.

I don't know
if I will ever find out
but what keeps coming to mind
is his request that I give the eulogy
at his wake.
I know he admires honesty
and always says
he is unafraid of the truth.
But I think, perhaps this is his way
of stacking the deck
in hopes
that I'll be honest
but not *too* honest
when the time comes.

Just Visiting

We fall in love
every time
she comes to town,
which isn't often,
just enough
to hold hands for the first time
once again,
smile and recognize
where we belong.

The trips are always too short,
and the clocks tick too loud.
Each meeting
we always agree
to share everything;
our words, feelings,
depth of emotions,
food, beers and bodies,
what-ifs, hopes and realities,
to leave nothing untouched.

However, the moment she is gone
a thousand unsaid words and phrases
appear in desperation,
fearful they will never be heard.
No forward plans
are ever made.
Only a whisper of
I will return.

When she drives away
before the sun rises,
I am devastated....again,

not able to take
watching her fade
into a day
I will not be part of.
So I go back to sleep
to dream
a different
ending.

NO
SMOKING
PRIVATE

Todd Cirillo was born of bastard lineage. He has many books and misdemeanors. His books include; *Sucker's Paradise, Burning the Evidence, ROXY, Three For the Road, Kisses From A Straight Razor*. He is co-founder and editor of Six Ft. Swells Press, and his poems have appeared in numerous national and international literary journals, magazines and on cocktail napkins everywhere. Articles with his particular take on existence have been featured in various national magazines. Todd lives in New Orleans, Louisiana where he seeks out shiny moments and strange wisdom.

He can be found at www.toddcirillo.com

"Todd Cirillo's new poetry collection DISPOSABLE DARLINGS is a celebration for those beautiful moments of living with no strings attached. Like a true pirate poet, Cirillo's poems pillage the senses with good music, stiff drinks, and even a little romance. Cirillo's strengths are on full display in this collection. Sit back with your favorite drink and enjoy. Welcome to the party."— Jake St. John, author of *Lost City Highway*

"What I love about Todd's poetry is its ability to make me laugh out loud, feel loved or heartbroken or like I've pre-gamed for a party I wasn't invited to but craved to be a part of. Reading DISPOSABLE DARLINGS creates a sensation that these poems happened to me. Todd is abundantly clever in his wordplay and metaphors, without being over the top. This is a book I read over and over again—while at a bar, traveling, in the park, stuck in traffic. Take a moment to read "Useful Poetry," because I strongly suggest you make good use of this book in typical and potentially suggestive ways, because I have, and I love every minute of it."— Linzi Garcia, author of *Thank You*

"Todd Cirillo's work is like that old friend who is always there at the bar to share a drink and some good laughs, and also make you think. It's work that to a certain degree always makes you feel good knowing it aims to entertain without preaching or having a hidden agenda. It's a good jukebox with excellent tunes and where an ice cold beer is waiting before you even take your seat. Todd doesn't speak at you as most so-called modern poets do in that pretentious sense he speaks to you as friend and connects as great writers should. His pages are his truth and he provides a much needed escape in times when that is needed more so than ever. Take the ride. I promise it will always be worth the price of admission."— John Patrick Robbins, Editor In Chief of the *Rye Whiskey Review*

MORE ROADSIDE PRESS TITLES:

By Plane, Train or Coincidence
Michele McDannold

Prying
Jack Micheline, Charles Bukowski and Catfish McDaris

Wolf Whistles Behind the Dumpster
Dan Provost

Busking Blues: Recollections of a Chicago Street Musician and Squatter
Westley Heine

Unknowable Things
Kerry Trautman

How to Play House
Heather Dorn

Kiss the Heathens
Ryan Quinn Flanagan

St. James Infirmary
Steven Meloan

Street Corner Spirits
Westley Heine

A Room Above a Convenience Store
William Taylor Jr.

Resurrection Song
George Wallace

Nothing and Too Much to Talk About
Nancy Patrice Davenport

MORE ROADSIDE PRESS TITLES:

Bar Guide for the Seriously Deranged
Alan Catlin

Born on Good Friday
Nathan Graziano

Under Normal Conditions
Karl Koweski

The Dead and the Desperate
Dan Denton

Clown Gravy
Misti Rainwater-Lites

Walking Away
Michael D. Grover

All in a Pretty Little Row
Dan Provost

These Are the People in Your Neighbourhood
Jordan Trethewey

They Said I Wasn't College Material
Scot Young

Radio Water
Francine Witte

And Blackberries Grew Wild
Susan Mickelberry

Licorice Heart
Miles Budimir